# PASSIVE INCOME

## 4 WAYS TO MAKE **MONEY** WHILE YOU **SLEEP**

FEMI AYANFE-OLUYE

## PASSIVE INCOME

## 4 Ways To Make Money While You Sleep!

This book is for informational and educational purpose. It is not intended for use as a source of legal, business, accounting or financial advice. All readers are advised to seek services of competent professionals for specific situations and areas of need.

The author does not assume any responsibility and disclaims any liability from the use of the content of this book. Kindly use your own discretion.

*Copyright © 2016 by Femi Ayanfe-Oluye*

ISBN-13: 978-1545212295

ISBN-10: 1545212295

## TABLE OF CONTENT

# CHAPTER 1

# TANKER OR PIPELINE?

*'The poor work for money while the rich have money work for them.'*

Ever wondered why the rich get richer and the poor get poorer?

One major reason is that the poor work for money while the rich have money work for them. While the poor work every day to make a living, the rich do the bulk of the work once and continue to reap the fruit of their work for a very long time.

By the time they get old, the poor man no longer has the same amount of energy as before and his productivity drops. This automatically affects his income and he begins to depend on others for survival.

The rich man on the other hand has been able to build several streams of passive income which keep bringing in money to him.

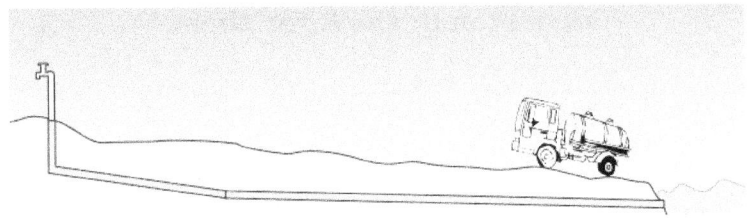

## Tanker or Pipeline?

I once heard the story of two men, Mr. Tank and Mr. Pipe. They stayed in a town where they had a water supply problem. The whole community usually goes to the river about ten kilometers from the town to get water.

Because of this arduous task, many of them resorted to buying water from water merchants. These two men were the only surviving water merchants in the town. Similar businesses had folded up as the business was not sustainable.

After much thought, Mr. Pipe decides there must be a way around this endless effort and set out to find a way out. Mr. Tank on the other hand continued to fetch 2 buckets per trip. After a while he increased his capacity to 10 buckets per trip with a trolley and eventually bought a tanker. Business was indeed booming.

Meanwhile, Mr. Pipe had concluded his findings and had started to construct a pipeline from the river to the town. In the meantime, he was supporting himself with the 2 buckets per trip as every extra fund had to go into the project.

After two years the project was concluded. His big reservoir in the town had been connected to the river through a series of pipes. With this constant supply of water he was able to reduce the price and the whole community started buying from him.

He also connected pipes to the homes of the rich people in the town who could afford to pay him periodically for this service.

Mr. Tank, on the other hand, was struggling to keep his customers. He decided he had to reduce his price as well. Eventually he could not reduce the price any further and the business was no longer sustainable.

He soon went out of business while Mr. Pipe works a few hours each day to inspect his reservoir business and does maintenance work on his pipes. He had money flowing in naturally.

The question I have for you is 'which one do you prefer? **Do you want to have a tanker or a pipeline?'** While one may be better, a combination of the two is the best. If one dries up or stops working, you have the other to fall back on.

You need to understand what passive income is and how to create yours today.

# CHAPTER 2

# WHAT IS PASSIVE INCOME?

*'The key thing in passive income is system.'*

This is income that you earn with little or no effort. It is often called residual income because the bulk of the work is done once while little extra effort may be required to keep it running. There are also some that require no additional effort. The money just keeps flowing.

Any work that involves your active participation cannot be regarded as passive income. Passive income is the revenue you get from your financial reserves or real assets that you have been able to create. The key thing in passive income is **system**.

You need to understand how it works and like Mr. Pipe, in our story, be able to systemize the process in such a way that you are left with little or no work to do.

## The Power of Passive Income

This kind of income is a good tool to use to build wealth. I must also warn at this point that having a passive income that continuously pump cash into your pocket does not mean you are wealthy.

Always remember Parkinson's Law that states that 'expense will always rise to meet up with income.' Even if you are earning a million dollars today, if you are not financially intelligent, you can still go broke. An increase in cash flow does not automatically translate to wealth. It is only an opportunity to build wealth.

The income from your passive income should be used to create more assets. You may choose to spend a part of it but the bulk should go back into creating more.

Even a farmer knows he must first separate the seed for the next planting season before he starts to eat from his harvest. The assurance of the next harvest is dependent on his ability to put some seed aside and replant in the next season. The more of these assets you have the wealthier you can become.

The income potential from many of them is also limitless. The extent to which you reproduce and earn depends on you. It may require a little effort from you to keep increasing it.

The good part is that with the little extra effort, your returns are huge. As long as the proper system is in place, you can keep increasing it with a multiplier effect on your earnings.

While there are several streams of passive income, we will only take a look at the most popular and most profitable of them. These are real estate, intellectual property, automated business and marketing.

# CHAPTER 3

# REAL ESTATE

*'The key thing about real estate is location.'*

This is the most popular and the most expensive. There is a great need for accommodation of various sorts. They range from residential houses to shopping and office complex. Others are hotels, event centers and other recreational resorts.

The initial work is the fund you invest as a number of them are quite expensive. You may also need to supervise the building or outsource it.

Subsequently you will need to be dealing with your tenants. This work can also be given out to real estate agents to manage for you. It has a few advantages over others which include:

1. **Rental Income:** Although it is capital intensive, the rewards are enormous. It comes in the form of rental income that the tenants pay you.

2. **Value appreciation:** In addition, the value of real estate is always on the rise. This capital appreciation in the value of the asset also increases the amount of rent you can charge.

3. **Financial leverage:** It also serves as a financial leverage as the properties could be used to secure loan facilities from banks.

The key thing about real estate is **location.** You need to carefully choose your location with foresight. You should estimate the potential gains vis-à-vis the cost to know whether it will be worth the while.

The location should also suit the kind of property you want to have with the necessary infrastructures and amenities in place to attract the potential tenants.

## 5 Ways to Make Money from Real Estate

1.      **Land Banking**

The value of land naturally appreciates. This is simply because the demand is more than the supply (which is finite).

A good alternative to leaving your money in the bank is to tie it down in a landed property. What you should be concerned about is your return on investment and the rate of capital appreciation.

## 2.     Farmland

With the continuous drop in the oil price, the attention is gradually shifting to agriculture. What you need for a farm is a vast expanse of land which exists in abundant supply especially in the suburbs.

You can get acres of land at cheap prices on which you can situate your farm. You can plant crops, economic trees or even go into animal farming. With a farmland, you earn income yearly while your land continues to appreciate in value.

## 3.     Buy and refurbish

If you do not have the patience and time for the two investments highlighted above, you can simply look out for properties that have been put up for sale for a number of reasons.

With proper due diligence, you can find good deals you can buy at a reasonable discount. You can refurbish the property and resell or lease out at a good profit margin.

4.      **Build and sell**

There are many young families today who want to own a home of theirs but don't want to go through the hassle of building. Choose a good location, preferably an estate and build a block of apartments. You may also get a few friends to pool funds together if you cannot afford the cost alone.

An easier route may be to sell some apartments at an off-plan rate (usually discounted). This would provide you with funds to complete the project after which you can sell the remaining apartments or share the proceeds based on your contribution.

5.      **Shops and offices**

SMEs are the mainstay of any economy and demand for shops and office spaces is always more than supply.

The key thing with this investment would be to choose a very good location where potential tenants can get good visibility and traffic. The rental payments could be a good source of consistent cash flow especially if their payment cycle is varied.

Alternatively, you can buy shops in shopping malls and lease or rent to small businesses at a mark-up.

# CHAPTER 4

# INTELLECTUAL PROPERTY

*'The key thing in intellectual property is content and originality.'*

This is another common one. While some are enjoying it many others do not understand it. The works of pirates have also discouraged many people from venturing into this area.

A proper understanding of the working and the legal input required in order to derive the best from your intellectual asset is crucial. Intellectual property is the creation of one's brain. It is used to refer to any work that a person has an original claim to.

The mind is a powerful tool and a major resource in the course of building wealth. Many ideas pass through your mind everyday that if you can just ponder on it a little more, can turn out to be a big product.

All the inventions and technological advancements that we have today are products of people's mind. Even the celebrities of today are people who decided to bring out the innate potential in them to create something useful.

The musicians, artists, authors, inventors, and many more have created for themselves assets which have the potential to bring in continuous income.

## 4 Main Types of Intellectual Property

1. **Copyrights:** These are legal protection for an author's work. Such works include literature, movies, documentaries, music, artwork, software etc. The copyright is automatically generated once the product is created, but can also be registered for increased protection.

2. **Trademarks:** These are legally distinguishable symbols of a business. They could be words, logos or a combination of the two. They are usually intangibles and need to be registered to claim the protection.

3. **Trade secrets:** Unlike trademarks which are just symbols, trade secrets are the unique internal dynamics of a business that are kept from public knowledge. These may include its systems, processes, formulas or recipes. They usually have economic value and need to be protected.

4. **Patents:** These are exclusive rights earned on an invention. It includes the right to tangibles such as products, designs or templates. The holder must prove that the innovation is his original work for him to earn this protection.

# 3 Ways to Make Money from Intellectual Property

## 1. Licensing

This involves transferring the right to use your intellectual property to someone else. It could be an exclusive right for the licensee to use the intellectual property within a region or for a specified period of time.

Licensing rights are given in exchange for royalties which are usually a small proportion of the revenue made from the use of the intellectual property. These can continue for as long as the contract stipulates.

## 2. Franchising

This involves allowing someone to leverage on your brand name and brand equity to launch and run their business. You would need to provide support and monitor compliance with procedural standards in order to maintain the quality you are already known for.

The franchisee usually pays a one-time fee to get this right or may be required to pay a percentage of yearly turnover as franchising fees. It could be a good way to scale your operations and take advantage of untapped markets.

## 3. Merchandising

This involves the outright sale or transfer of right to an intellectual property to another person. This is usually common with very creative people that do not have the resources or are not interested in developing their idea further.

Some people focus on creating products for others businesses, while some others get to sell the intellectual property when they cannot see future value in it. The revenue received from such sale can be invested in another business or used in creating another product.

The key thing in intellectual property is **content** and **originality**. People pay for good products and anything they enjoy.

You also get to earn more when you prove that you can reproduce the same thing over again. The raw material you need is your mind which you already have.

What separates these people from the rest is the amount of time they are willing to spend to work on their mind and develop the skill.

The truth is that you do not have to be born with the skill. While some people's skill is as a result of nature, others nurtured the passion and learnt the skill.

# CHAPTER 5

# AUTOMATED BUSINESS

*'Business does not have to be subsistence. You can build a business up such that it runs by itself. The secret to this is automation.'*

Business is attractive but the reality of the work scares many a people. This is often because of their perception of business.

Many people in business are simply self-employed. While they left their jobs to start a business and get some freedom, they end up with another job. They suddenly discover that they have to do a lot of things to keep the business running.

This gets them so engrossed that they never really get the freedom they long sought. These businesses cannot survive without the active participation of the owners and eventually fold up as soon as the owners leave.

Business does not have to be subsistence. You can build a business up such that it runs by itself. The secret to this is **automation**.

Automation allows you to have a business while you still keep your 9-5 job or do other things that are important to you.

We need to remove our mind from the mentality that we must sit and monitor our business otherwise someone will cheat us.

Step up and begin to find out what you need to do to keep it as an entity independent of you. In minding your business, you need to put your mind (not your body) to work.

# 3 Ways to Automate Your Business

## 1. Systems

A system is anything that saves you space, time, energy and money. You need to document how every part of the business runs so that even if you are not there, someone else can keep it going.

*'Great organizations run on systems and if you want your business to be great you have to systemize it.'*

A system is like a food recipe that allows anyone to cook the same menu. This is possible because the details of the work had been outlined in the cookery book.

The same applies to business; you need to design the system before commencing the operation. As the operations proceed, you will need to update your system to reflect other things you may have omitted.

Great organizations run on systems and if you want your business to be great you have to systemize it.

## 2. People

People are also crucial to the business. You do not have all the skills and knowledge for the work. Even if you do, you cannot do everything because of your limitation of time.

*'Delegation allows you to major on your strengths and crucial parts of the business while others take care of the rest.'*

This is where many entrepreneurs get stuck and cannot grow further because time will not allow them.

Assess your human resource needs appropriately and learn to delegate. This will free up your time for more strategic things. It will also free your mind to think of ways to improve your business.

Delegation allows you to major on your strengths and crucial parts of the business while others take care of the rest.

## 3. Technology

With technological advancement, many mundane things can now be performed by machines. Furthermore, information and communication technology has also eased the means of doing business.

The coming of the internet has now made the world a global village in such a way that you can do business with anyone in any part of the world at the speed of thought.

Spend money on technology as it will save you time and reduce your overhead cost. Find out areas of your business where you can apply automation and move your business to the next level.

The income from automated business comes in the form of:

1. **Profit:** As a result of automation, you will be able to keep your cost low while improving efficiency. This will naturally translate into more profit.

2. **Time:** Time is indeed money. You also have your time saved up for other productive ventures. Once you have mastered the art, you can

reproduce and start as many businesses as you have capacity for.

3. **Director's bonus:** By sitting on the board of the several businesses you own, you are entitled to director's bonus and all the other pecks that come with ownership. The more the businesses, the more the cash flow.

# CHAPTER 6

# MARKETING

*'The key thing in marketing is to do your due diligence to be sure of the kind of company you are recommending.'*

This word sends vibes down the nerves of some people. Marketing is simply informing the market and getting the market to buy.

We live in the market everyday and have daily interactions with it. The market is you and I. You buy products from time to time and pay for services in one way or the other. In this instance you are the market.

The market is the whole world since no one lives independent of the other. Every time you buy a product or pay for a service, you are exchanging your money for the value someone created.

Since tastes differ and preferences change, we do not use the same product or service forever. Marketing is getting the market to be favorably disposed to a particular product or service to the extent that they exchange their money for its value.

Before you begin to figure it as something difficult, let me remind you that you do it every day.

Ever thought of how many times you have recommended a product or someone's service? Were you ever paid for it?

While you enjoyed value from the product and was so excited that you informed someone else, the producer simply smiles to the bank alone. The viral referral and patronage that he receives makes him rich while you get nothing for it.

## 2 Major Ways to Earn Passive Income from Marketing

### 1. Network marketing

This is one business that has been mostly misunderstood. While I empathize with those who have had their fingers burnt, I will say that it is still a very viable income stream.

I should also state that this is different from pyramid schemes or 'ponzi'. A real network marketing company has a legitimate product or service they sell.

The network marketing route is just a marketing option that they chose to use to promote their products. There are several types from the unilevel to the multilevel and from the binary to the board systems.

You earn a bonus whenever you get someone else to buy into the company. You also earn whenever someone in your team makes a sale.

Thus, it promotes team work and the building of a network which you are also rewarded for. There are also several other benefits that you are entitled to as you rise through the ranks.

## 2. Affiliate marketing

This is quite different from network marketing. With affiliate marketing, you do not need to build any network or team.

You serve as an agent for the company and get paid for your direct effort. While most pay you only for the sales you make, some others pay you for the leads you generate also.

It is more common on the internet, but offline businesses are also beginning to adopt this marketing style.

The income comes in the form of commission or bonus. You earn only from your direct effort and no one shares your reward with you.

These two marketing businesses are the cheapest form of passive income to go into. They also allow the marketer to focus on getting sales as there are proper systems in place to assist in getting results.

The key thing in this business is to do your **due diligence** to be sure of the kind of company you are recommending. This will also determine your ability to earn for a long period while maintaining your integrity.

Since you talk to people every day, thus selling your opinion and idea on issues, sales should not be a big deal. Just do some extra work in learning the ropes and add it to your everyday conversation as it takes only a little extra from you.

# CHAPTER 7

# YOUR PLAN

*'Action is what separates winners from losers'*

Do you remember our story at the beginning of this book? Unlike Mr. Tank, do not wait till competition throws you out of business or your pay check stops coming. Start to earn from a passive income stream today.

You can major on any one that appeals to you the most or combine them as you like. The bottom line is that you must earn money from these opportunities that consume less time and energy.

Do not sit down with only your active income. The residual nature of the passive income streams can help you realize your dream of sustainable wealth faster and better. Write your plan today

1) How many streams of passive income do you earn from? List them.

_____

_____

_____

_____

_____

_____

_____

_____

_____

_____

_____

_____

_____

_____

_____

_____

2) How many streams do you want to start earning from? List them.

_____

_____

_____

_____

_____

_____

_____

_____

_____

_____

_____

_____

_____

_____

_____

_____

3) Where can you get information or assistance on them? Internet, investment clubs, seminars...

_____

_____

_____

_____

_____

_____

_____

_____

_____

_____

_____

_____

_____

_____

_____

4) How much time do you want to dedicate to it?

_____

_____

_____

_____

_____

_____

_____

_____

_____

_____

_____

_____

_____

_____

_____

_____

5) Why do you want this stream of passive income?

_____

_____

_____

_____

_____

_____

_____

_____

_____

_____

_____

_____

_____

_____

_____

6) When will you start? NOW!

_____

_____

_____

_____

_____

_____

_____

_____

_____

_____

_____

_____

_____

_____

_____

_____

_____

## About the Author

Hi, my name is Femi Ayanfe-Oluye, and I am a FEMI (Financial Educator, Manager and Investor). I have a passion, purpose and pursuit, to build sustainable wealth in people, organizations and nations. You are welcome as you join me on this mission.

You may subscribe to my website: Strategic Financial Management (www.ayanfeoluye.com)

Email: femi@ayanfeoluye.com

Or follow on social media:

Facebook.com/ayanfeoluye

Twitter: @ayanfeoluye


I would love to hear from you.

Thank you.

## **Other Books by the Author**

Get simple strategies you can use to DOUBLE your income while on that JOB!

What you would find inside this handbook:

- 6 ways to manage and convert your INCOME into ASSETS.

- 3 SOCIAL CAPITAL in your job you can use to your ADVANTAGE

- 3 PROFESSIONAL ASSETS you can leverage to increase your VALUE

Your job should be LEVERAGE not an end in itself. There is more VALUE in that job than you might have realized. Get your copy NOW!

Get simple strategies you can use to make your money WORK for you and PRODUCE MORE MONEY while you face your job or business!

What you would find inside this handbook:

- 6 reasons why your MONEY SHOULD WORK FOR YOU rather than you working for money all your life
- 5 ASSETS you should have in your PORTFOLIO
- 10 BENEFITS of owning PAPER ASSETS

Money should be your MESSENGER and not your MASTER. Learn how to make the money you have worked for to start working for you. Get your copy NOW!

Get simple strategies you can use to PROFIT from the NEW 'REAL ESTATE' of the 21ST CENTURY called the INTERNET

What you would find inside this handbook:

- 6 reasons why the INTERNET is the NEW 'REAL ESTATE'
- 5 HIGHLY SCALABLE businesses you can do on the WEB
- 7 FUTURE TRENDS you can POSITION yourself for and be a TRAILBLAZER

The world has MOVED! The earlier you realized and woke up, the better. Learn how to PROFIT from this 'REAL ESTATE' that has NO PHYSICAL BOUNDARIES. Get your copy NOW!

MULTIPLE INCOME

HOW TO BE A 'JACK' OF ALL **TRADES** AND A 'MASTER' OF ALL

FEMI AYANFE-OLUYE

Get simple strategies you can use to MAXIMIZE the business of your talents, skills and opportunities AT THE SAME TIME.

What you would find inside this handbook:

- 6 ways to IDENTIFY what you HAVE and CAN DO
- 3 ways you can TURN what you have and can do into a BUSINESS
- 3 ways to SCALE your businesses and MULTIPLY your CAPACITY

In this world of uncertainties, it is not advisable to put all your eggs in ONE BASKET. Learn how you can be a 'JACK' OF ALL TRADES and still master everything with EASE. Get your copy NOW!

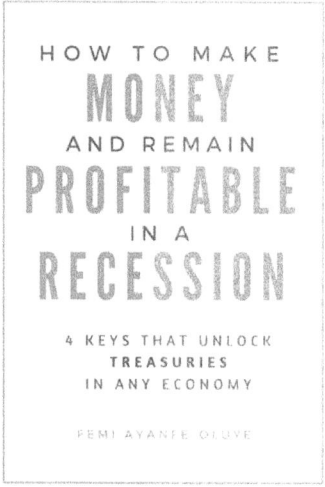

This book will show you why many cry and only a few smile during recessions.

In this book, you will discover:

- 7 Things everybody must do in a recession TO MAKE MONEY.
- 6 things every business must do TO REMAIN PROFITABLE.
- The 4 Keys that UNLOCK TREASURIES in any economy – Recession or not!

Many lost millions in the last recession. Your little investment to gain this KNOWLEDGE would save you untold financial loss and make you SEE what others do not see. Get your copy NOW!